Disney MOVIE MAGIC

A piano accompaniment book (HL00841181) is available for this collection.

ISBN 978-0-7935-7840-5

HAL•LEONARD®
CORPORATION
7777 W. BLUEMOUND RD. P.O. BOX 13819 MILWAUKEE, WI 53213

Visit Hal Leonard Online at
www.halleonard.com

OUT OF THIN AIR
from Walt Disney's ALADDIN AND THE KING OF THIEVES

Violin

Words and Music by
DAVID FRIEDMAN

CAN YOU FEEL THE LOVE TONIGHT

from Walt Disney Pictures' THE LION KING

Violin

Music by ELTON JOHN
Lyrics by TIM RICE

CIRCLE OF LIFE

from Walt Disney Pictures' THE LION KING

Violin

Music by ELTON JOHN
Lyrics by TIM RICE

5

HAKUNA MATATA

from Walt Disney Pictures' THE LION KING

Music by ELTON JOHN
Lyrics by TIM RICE

Violin

I JUST CAN'T WAIT TO BE KING

from Walt Disney Pictures' THE LION KING

Violin

Music by ELTON JOHN
Lyrics by TIM RICE

THIS LAND

from Walt Disney Pictures' THE LION KING

Violin

Music by
HANS ZIMMER

THE VIRGINIA COMPANY

from Walt Disney's POCAHONTAS

Violin

Music by ALAN MENKEN
Lyrics by STEPHEN SCHWARTZ

COLORS OF THE WIND
from Walt Disney's POCAHONTAS

Violin

Music by ALAN MENKEN
Lyrics by STEPHEN SCHWARTZ

D.S. al Coda

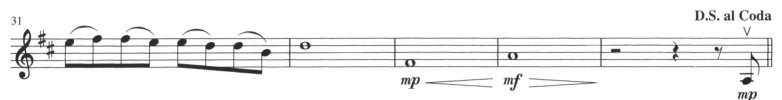

CODA

JUST AROUND THE RIVERBEND

from Walt Disney's POCAHONTAS

Violin

Music by ALAN MENKEN
Lyrics by STEPHEN SCHWARTZ

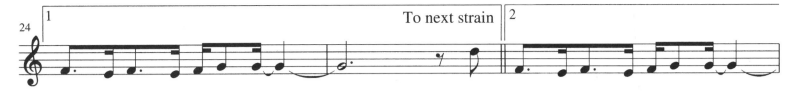

To next strain

To Coda ⊕

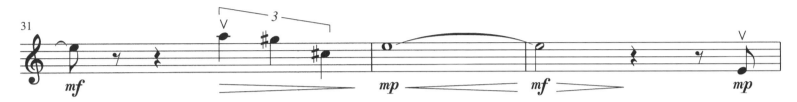

D.S. al Coda

⊕ CODA

Meno mosso - freely

Piu mosso

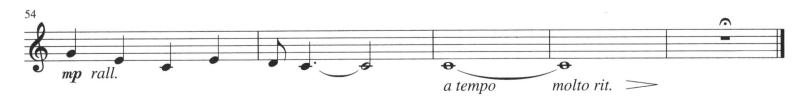

MINE, MINE, MINE
from Walt Disney's POCAHONTAS

Violin

Music by ALAN MENKEN
Lyrics by STEPHEN SCHWARTZ

CRUELLA DE VIL
from Walt Disney's 101 DALMATIANS

Violin

Words and Music by
MEL LEVEN

FORGET ABOUT LOVE

from Walt Disney's THE RETURN OF JAFAR

Violin

Words and Music by
MICHAEL SILVERSHER and PATTY SILVERSHER

Freely

YOU'VE GOT A FRIEND IN ME

from Walt Disney's TOY STORY

Violin

Music and Lyrics by
RANDY NEWMAN

STRANGE THINGS
from Walt Disney's TOY STORY

Violin

Music and Lyrics by
RANDY NEWMAN